TELLING
THE ROSARY

VINCENT SHERLOCK

First published in 2019 by Messenger Publications

ISBN: 978 1 78812 107 1

Designed by Messenger Publications Design Department
Typeset in Stevens Tilting Pro, LTC Caslon
Printed by Johnswood Press Ltd

Messenger Publications,
37 Lower Leeson Street, Dublin 2
www.messenger.ie

CONTENTS

Introduction : 5

CHAPTER 1: THE JOYFUL MYSTERIES ~ 7

CHAPTER 2: THE LUMINOUS MYSTERIES ~ 20

INTRODUCTION

I n Dick Farrelly's iconic song, 'The Isle of Innisfree',
an emigrant reflects on his memories of home. He
misses all that was familiar to him. Things that remain
embedded in his memory. Among his most cherished
memories, is that of family prayer and his description is
wonderful:

> *And then into a humble shack I wander*
> *my dear old home, and tenderly behold*
> *the folks I love around the turf fire gathered*
> *on bended knees their Rosary is told.*

It is said that Farrelly got the idea for this song when
travelling by bus from Co. Meath to Dublin. I have an
image of him scribbling down the lines lest he'd forget
them. I wonder whether this scene of family prayer was
part of that original bus-penned draft, but even if it wasn't,
I am so pleased it found its way into the song he released.

'On bended knee their Rosary is told' is truly an
inspired description of the Rosary's place in our story of

faith. He could have said the Rosary was 'said', 'recited' or 'prayed' but no, the verb he used is the past tense of 'to tell'. The Rosary then, as he sees it, is the telling of a story, and so it is.

What is that story? It's the story of Christ – told from Gabriel's visit to Mary in the first joyful mystery of the Annunciation, right through to the second glorious mystery of the Ascension, followed by the fulfilment of the Lord's promise that he would send to us 'An Advocate', as prayed in the third glorious mystery, 'The Descent of the Holy Spirit'.

In the following pages maybe we could look at that story as it is 'told' in the Rosary. Maybe we will get a phrase or two to wrap around the Our Father, ten Hail Marys and Glory Be. A thought or two to accompany us as we take the beads in hand.

Of course, the Rosary when fully told, begins with the creed. This has always to be our starting place. *We acknowledge our belief in the central teachings of our faith; God is creator of Heaven and earth, Jesus was born for us, lived among and died for us. He rose from the dead and sits at God's right hand. The Holy Spirit, together with Father and Son, in that mystery of Trinity, continues to be a guiding hand in all our lives. We acknowledge too, our faith in the Catholic Church, in life after death and in the resurrection.*

This part of our story must also be told and sits easily in the prayer we call 'The Rosary'.

CHAPTER 1
THE JOYFUL MYSTERIES

*Ordinarily these mysteries are prayed
on Monday and Saturday.*

The Joyful Mysteries bring us through the early part of the life of Jesus, from the moment his impending birth is announced to Mary to the time he is found in the Temple, having been missing for a number of days.

They speak to us of relationships between people and how we can so often receive and give support. For this to happen, people must be willing to encounter one another, even in uncertain circumstances.

Family life is at the heart of these mysteries and the relationship within family is presented as the key ingredient of all relationships. Mary's relationship with Joseph, her cousin Elizabeth and her willingness to engage with Simeon and Anna all speak of a woman who knows the value of love and support in her life. Sometimes joy is found after sadness and uncertainty as evidenced in the final Joyful Mystery – 'The Finding of the Child Jesus in the Temple'.

Openness to God's will leads us truly to a place of joy, and that place is celebrated in the joyful mysteries.

JOYFUL MYSTERY 1
THE ANNUNCIATION
(LK 1:26–38)

Who Is in the Story?
Gabriel, the Archangel, Mary and Elizabeth are the main characters here. Joseph, of course, is in the background as is Zechariah.

The Story Told
St Luke's Gospel tells us the story behind this mystery of the Rosary. There is a lot of detail in the passage. We are told where Gabriel, the archangel was to visit, who he visited, to whom she was engaged; we are given the name of her elderly cousin and some of that cousin's story is also shared, not least that she is in her sixth month of pregnancy, despite having reached old age. We are told about a town in the 'Hill country of Judah', about a girl called Mary who was engaged to Joseph. It is a very personal story. God knows who he is dealing with and with whom he wants to communicate.

In many ways that is the story this mystery is telling. It is asking us to know Mary and to know her people and situation and to hear, in her voice, the uncertainty versed in the question: 'But how can this be?' The question is answered, and the reassurance is given. The answer is heeded, and the reassurance accepted. This leads Mary to that point where she can truly say: 'I am the handmaid of the Lord, let what you have said be done to me' (Lk 1:38).

What story is this mystery telling? It is telling a story that is unfolding in all our lives where we must face news that may or may not be welcome. Maybe it is news of sickness, either in ourselves or someone very dear to us. It might be news about a job offer or a redundancy, an opportunity or a set-back. The key is to search for God in the news announced, and to see how best we can align ourselves with his will, even if we do not fully grasp or understand it. This mystery encourages us to ask: 'how can this be?' and to be open to hearing, in time, the fullness of God's explanation. Part of the story too, is reminding us that our names and the names of those for whom we might pray in this mystery are important to and known by God. 'I have called you by name, you are mine' (Isa 43:1).

Thoughts for Prayer
There is room here for a bit of reflection on God's will in our lives. How open are we to changing course, should God ask something of us? A prayer to recognise the Angel of Opportunity that God may send in our direction and to have an open ear and open heart. Possibly a prayer too for the ability to focus our attention on what is being said so that we might better respond. Maybe there's room for gratitude too, for the times we have sensed and been aware of God communicating with us.

JOYFUL MYSTERY 2
THE VISITATION
(LK 1:39–45)

Who Is in the Story?
The cousins, Mary and Elizabeth and the unborn cousins, Jesus and John the Baptist.

The Story Told
All the mysteries of the Rosary do not flow as easily from one bible verse to another, but this mystery continues from the Annunciation. There, Mary was told that her elderly cousin was in her sixth month of pregnancy and, in this mystery, Mary goes to be with her.

It is such a natural response and one this mystery wants us to value. The importance of supporting people in their hour of need is at the heart of the Christian message. The encounter between Mary and Elizabeth reveals something of their deep faith and of their connectedness. Without a word being said by Mary, Elizabeth recognises her as the mother-to-be of the Messiah – 'Why should I be honoured with a visit from the mother of my Lord? For the moment your greeting reached my ear … ' (Lk 1:43).

A conversation follows between the two and there is a clear recognition that a power greater than either is at work. This leads Mary to draw from words of the Old Testament in her praise of God and in her acknowledgement of her own feelings of unworthiness. The visitation leads to prayer and the joined acceptance of a mission. These two women, and the children they carry, are destined to be part of a story told to this day.

In this mystery we might well reflect on our own visitation to people's homes and of visits made to our homes. What conversations take place? Are they rooted in friendship or can they slip into occasions of gossip? When we visit other people, what is it we want to bring? What is it we wish or need to achieve? Why did Mary visit Elizabeth? Chances are there were a few reasons, among them perhaps, Mary needing time away to clear her own thoughts but, even more importantly to be with someone who needed her.

Finally, we are told that Mary stayed with Elizabeth about three months before she returned home. In other words, she stayed with Elizabeth until her child was born – for as long as she was needed. Maybe we could pray here for that same gift of time – to be with people and in situations for as long as we are needed.

Thoughts for Prayer

Maybe a prayer at this mystery, this chapter of the story, around our own visitations. Is there a visit we have been putting off for some reason? A visit that needs to be made. It may well be to a grave or a church or to someone that, for too long, we have promised to visit but have not quite got around to it. Pray in this mystery for a genuine desire to make time to visit – to go where you are needed. A remembrance as well of Mary and Elizabeth's grasp of their own faith and of the unfolding of God's plan. Maybe we could pray in this mystery for a deeper awareness of our own faith and of Scripture that we can draw from both when we need guidance and a deeper understanding of a situation.

JOYFUL MYSTERY 3
THE NATIVITY
(LK 2:1-20)

Who Is in the Story?
Directly we meet Jesus, Mary and Joseph – the Holy Family. Alongside them, others are mentioned or alluded to, among these: the innkeeper, the shepherds on the nearby hill, the angels and, in time the Wise Men.

The Story Told
It is a story of travel and uncertainty where Joseph and Mary are in strange surrounds, without resources or the security of a place to call their own. Added to this, Mary is about to give birth and the lack of safe lodging is a genuine concern. Eventually shelter is offered and gratefully accepted, and the scene is set for the birth of Jesus. Mary and Joseph are alone and without the support of family and friends. They are presented as a dependant couple, and the image of Jesus being born in a borrowed shed is one that calls us to an awareness of people's needs. Our gratitude, in this mystery, is with the innkeeper who found, in the depths of his heart, the 'yes' that Mary found in the depths of hers and gave what he was able to give.

The shepherds, going about their daily work, stand as a reminder to us that our daily work and routine should never come between us and hearing the fullness of God's message. Attentive to the voice of angels, we never know at what moment we might be asked to alter course to answer God's call. The angel's message 'Do not be afraid' is one that is found many times in the pages of Scripture and yet we can, all too often, find ourselves paralysed by fear.

We hear also, from among their own number, one find his voice: 'Let us go and see this thing we have been told about' (Lk 1:15) and, hearing his words, they leave their sheep. Doing so was, not alone the appropriate response to the received message, but also a blessing to the shepherds – one and all. It is appropriate that shepherds were among the first to greet the newborn child who would, in time, be both shepherd and lamb. Their presence in the Christmas shed reminds us of the love the Lord has for us all and of his desire to lead us to safe and secure pastures.

Mention of the animals is also significant and is a reminder to us that all God's creation and creatures have a role to play and are deserving of respect. There is an appropriateness about the animals breathing warmth on the Christ child. The donkey and the cow have their place and it is no coincidence that later, it is on a donkey that the Messiah enters the final chapter of his earthly ministry as he heads for Jerusalem.

There is a lot going on in this mystery and the simplicity of the shed, reminds us that our faith does not have to be elaborate or complicated but rather rooted in a willingness to offer what we have so that a difference may be made.

Thoughts for Prayer
We could give thanks here for our own birth and for our parents, and all who were part of the story of our birth. We may know of some of them but others may have passed from memory, but it could be good to give thanks here for doctors, nurses, midwives, members of the Emergency Services who all can have a part to play in the delivery of a baby. Sadly some people have lost babies at the moment of birth so maybe a prayer too for grieving parents. Again, remembering the innkeeper, we might pray for a generous spirit and pray in thanks for those who have shown us kindness on occasions. The shepherds represent the man and woman on the street and in the workplace and we pray for an openness to God's message in all places, circumstances and times.

JOYFUL MYSTERY 4
THE PRESENTATION IN THE TEMPLE
(LK 2:22–40)

Who Is in the Story?
In addition to the Holy Family of Jesus, Mary and Joseph, the two people highlighted in this mystery are Simeon and Anna.

The Story Told

Mary and Joseph, in honouring their faith tradition, take their son to offer him to the Lord. This is a gesture of gratitude to God for the delivery of their son and a sign of handing on the faith. They follow carefully the teachings of the Law and bring with them the prescribed offerings.

In the temple, as well as encountering God, they meet two elderly people: Anna and Simeon. We are given some relevant information about both. Anna is a prayer-filled and committed church woman who spends much of her time in prayer and worship in the temple. Here she found consolation, following her husband's death after just seven years of marriage. Simeon, an old man, prayed that he would see the Messiah and had been assured that he would not die without that happening. He believed the authenticity of that promise and lived in hope of its fulfilment.

There is a lengthy exchange between the characters of this decade and the story told is one of respect between the generations. In many ways, this mystery is a model of Church where people of all ages gather, as one, to be together in faith and prayer. There is a trust displayed in this mystery where Joseph and Mary realise and accept this pair has something to share with them and a message that needs to be heard and heeded. Simeon recognises in the child what many – possibly even Joseph and Mary – had not fully realised; that he was in the presence of his saviour.

He prayed aloud and let it be known that God could take him anytime he wanted since the promise had been kept and he had indeed set his eyes on the Christ. This prayer is prayed every night all over the world in the Night Prayer of The Church and it comes directly from this moment and the story told in this mystery.

Anna too spoke to Mary and, from her own awareness of sorrow, foretold that Mary would endure hardship along the way. It was not so much a warning or a threat as a reassurance that, with and in faith, Mary would cope as Anna herself had coped and that she would find strength through her awareness of God's plan.

This is a very powerful mystery of the Rosary and one that we could spend much time with. Take it bit by bit, recognise the young couple doing what was expected of them. Recognise the fidelity and experience of the aged who have been travelling the road for many years and recognise too the trust that should exist in church where people can meet strangers who change the course of their lives.

Thoughts for Prayer

Gratitude again for our own parents who brought us to church for baptism and to them and our teachers who helped prepare us for the sacraments. We could think as well about our own understanding of our faith traditions and why we do certain things at a given time. For parents, this might be a mystery to reflect on how well the faith is being handed on to children and for some of our older people, this mystery could well be a reminder of the value they have in the lives of others. A prayer to accept where we are on the road of faith and to know that we are as one, in Church. Simeon and Anna longed to know more of Christ and were not afraid of death. Simeon's prayer, in particular, might well be a launching pad for our own prayer around the final things and a call to be focused on recognising God at work in our midst.

JOYFUL MYSTERY 5
THE FINDING OF THE CHILD JESUS IN THE TEMPLE
(LK 2:41–52)

Who Is in the Story?
While people are not named, we are reminded that Joseph and Mary had their family circle and it is among them they are found in this mystery. The doctors of the Law and learned people mentioned, remind us that those in authority too are called to encounter Jesus.

The Story Told
At twelve years of age, following a visit to Jerusalem and on the return journey, Joseph and Mary realise that Jesus is missing. Searching for him first among their own relations, they realise he is not with them. Terror sets in, and they return to Jerusalem in search of their son. The search is frantic and their hearts are broken. Eventually they find Jesus in the temple, sitting among the doctors of the Law and the learned people who are amazed at the wisdom spoken by this young child. Mary rushes to

Jesus, grabs him and leaves him in no doubt that what he has done is wrong and that he has caused great worry to her and Joseph. Jesus tells her there was no need for them to worry and adds: 'Did you not know that I must be about my father's business?'(Lk 2:49). It's a moment of recognition perhaps, for Mary and Joseph, that their son is marked out for something special and something that will, in time, take Jesus away from them in a way they could not imagine. The hope is that Mary will remember that all he does is in accordance with the Father's business.

The role of the doctors of the Law is a reminder that many of these same people or their successors, fail to grasp fully who is speaking to them. Their admiration of the child is not enough twenty years later when the man is again before them and they fail to be impressed or open to what he has to say. The words of the child astounded them, but the message of the man frightened them. Their being spellbound gave way to their being jealous and uncertain. They forgot the boy and, unlike Simeon, just looked at what was before them rather than the future contained in the boy. They had ears to hear his words but not Simeon's eyes to see who was in their midst.

Jerusalem will have another day – another chance to realise who is in its midst but on this occasion, ones who could have noticed, fell that bit short and an opportunity to meet and recognise the Messiah was missed.

We are told that Jesus returned home with Mary and Joseph and lived under their authority, all the while growing in wisdom and maturity.

Thoughts for Prayer

In an age when we hear so much of children going missing, we might pray here for parents who must face that awful reality and whose lives are torn asunder. We might too remember children who though not physically lost, can often go through lengthy periods often being spiritually missing and sometimes are not found. This too can be a source of heartbreak for parents. The fact that Jesus was found in the temple could be a focus for our prayer as well and that we stand a better chance of finding Jesus in a place of worship and surrounded by worshipping people. This mystery is again an opportunity to pray for our parents and family circle – remembering that Mary and Joseph's relations were also involved in the search and in the care of Jesus.

CHAPTER 2
THE LUMINOUS MYSTERIES

Ordinarily these mysteries are prayed on Thursday.

In 2002, Pope St John Paul II added these mysteries to the Rosary. In so doing, he wanted to bridge the gap that existed between the joyful mysteries which take us to the point where Jesus is a twelve-year-old boy and the sorrowful mysteries which tell us of the final days of Jesus' public ministry.

These mysteries are also called 'The Mysteries of Light' and take us through some of the Gospel stories recounting Jesus' ministry and his certain role as 'The Light of The World.' These mysteries then, help us to reflect on the light Jesus brought to our world through his various encounters with people.

As a piece, they bring us to an awareness of Jesus' desire to interact with people, to affirm them and be with them in their various needs. Through these mysteries, Jesus is revealed to us as one who assists people in their time of need (Cana) and one who seeks to draw all into a deeper realisation of his identity (Transfiguration).

LUMINOUS MYSTERY 1
THE BAPTISM OF THE LORD
(MT 3:13-17)

Who Is in the Story?

There are many people on the fringes but central to the story we find Jesus and his cousin, John the Baptist. The Father and Holy Spirit also feature in a significant way.

The Story Told

John the Baptist prepared the way for Jesus. He had leapt in his mother's womb when Jesus, also in the womb, was brought into his presence, and never failed to draw people to a deeper place of awareness. He preached the forgiveness of sins, about the need for personal conversion and lived what he preached. His lifestyle was austere and his mission vital. He sought, through all he said and did, to remind people that salvation was promised and possible but that it had to be chosen. He prepared the way of the Lord.

This caused some confusion too, as people began to think he might be the messiah. Indeed he was asked about this and reassured those asking that there was one coming after him, whose sandals he was not fit to untie. Confusion remained nonetheless and disciples formed around him. He was the one who pointed Jesus out to the first apostles when he said: 'There goes the lamb of God' and they followed Jesus, asking the crucial question; 'Where do you live?' that brought the equally important response: 'Come and see' (Jn 1:39).

Now John is baptising people in the River Jordan and

is approached by Jesus who requests baptism. Initially John refuses, saying that it is he who should receive baptism from Jesus but Jesus insists: 'For now, let it be this way' and John agrees. As soon as Jesus is baptised, the skies open and the Holy Spirit descends in the form of a dove and the voice of the Father is heard: 'This is my son, the beloved. My favour rests on him'.

This mystery then is central and raises the moment of our baptism to new heights. It is, for all baptised people, the moment when Father, Son and Holy Spirit – as one – enter our lives and make a promise to remain there. Baptism is about accepting God in our lives and being better people through that acceptance.

John said at one stage: 'He must increase and I must decrease'. From this moment there is little mention of John the Baptist in the Scriptures – apart from one or two questions put to Jesus about him. Jesus, however, leaves people in no doubt, that of all the people born, none greater than John ever existed.

We are told that the waters of baptism, as presented in this mystery and ever since, have been made holy by the one baptised.

Thoughts for the Prayer

A pause for reflection on our own baptism. Prayers for those who were there – parents, sponsor, priest, brothers, sisters and relatives. Maybe we could find out details we are not sure about so that we'd have a fairly clear account of our own baptism. Remember also, parents who today choose or perhaps don't choose baptism for their children.

Pray that there might be an increased awareness of the significance of this sacrament and its place in setting us on the journey of faith. Baptism is called 'The gateway to the sacraments' and it is only through that gateway we can travel into the fullness of faith and reception of the sacraments. This mystery might be a good place to reflect on and pray for an increased appreciation of what it means to request baptism – either for a child or for oneself in adult life. Finally, we might remember those who have not the opportunity to receive baptism due to not hearing the story of Christ and we could ask that present day John the Baptists might be sent their way to prepare them to encounter and choose Christ.

LUMINOUS MYSTERY 2
THE WEDDING FEAST OF CANA
(JN 2:1–12)

Who Is in the Story?
Though unnamed, we have the young couple at the heart of the story. Mary, Jesus and his disciples, the servants and the chief-steward.

The Story Told
It is listed as the first of the miracles of Jesus and is a gospel passage frequently used at wedding ceremonies. It is easy to see why that is the case since here Jesus works a wonder for a young couple celebrating marriage and

that is the hope for all couples on their wedding day – that Jesus will bless and multiply their happiness. On this occasion, the couple had invited Jesus and Mary to their wedding as well as some of his disciples. The story is very familiar to us and we know that the couple – perhaps even unknown to themselves – were facing embarrassment as they were about to run out of wine.

It is noteworthy that it was Mary who noticed this and brought it to Jesus' attention. This speaks to the mother in Mary who would not want to see her children embarrassed in any way. 'They have no wine', she whispers to Jesus and his response seems harsh: 'Woman, why turn to me. My hour has not come yet'. She says no more to him but speaks to the servants and says 'Do whatever he tells you'. There is trust here – Mary knows that Jesus will not turn a blind eye to the couple's need. This re-enforces for us the role of Mary as intercessor and explains why often we make our prayer through her. It is always Jesus who answers our prayer but Mary's role is very much recognised in this mystery.

What happens next is well documented. Jesus asks the servants to fill the water jars and they fill them 'to the brim'. That's an interesting point because it would have been easier for them to half fill the jars but, for some reason, they filled them to the brim. This lets us know that the more we are willing to put into life – to give to Jesus – the more we will receive. Without fuss or drama, the filled jars are found to contain wine – wine the chief steward declares to be the best wine of the night.

This miracle is recorded as the first of Jesus' miracles – a moment he let his glory be seen and his disciples believed in him. We are not told how the couple re-acted since it is likely they remained unaware that a miracle had happened around and for them. That is the way God seeks to operate in our lives and sometimes, the gift he gives us may well go unnoticed or be taken for granted.

Thoughts for Prayer

We might remember here relatives recently married or preparing for marriage. We might pray that couples continue to invite Jesus into their married life and family relationships and not lose sight of his presence. Mary's role as intercessor is also something we might reflect on in this mystery and remember that it is through her intercession that many of our prayers are brought into God's presence. Mary never seeks to be the worker of miracles or the responder to our prayer. Always, she seeks to point us in the direction of Jesus. May we remember in this mystery that sometimes we may not even know our needs but that Mary has a real and motherly concern for all her children and spots our needs – reminding Jesus that we have 'no wine' – whatever that wine represents. In this mystery we are asked to trust in God's providence and, having received from it, to be ever grateful that we are cared for. Finally we might pray that we would never take for granted acts of kindness or fail in our gratitude.

LUMINOUS MYSTERY 3
THE PROCLAMATION OF THE KINGDOM
(MK 1:15)

Who Is in the Story?

Here it gets a little crowded! For, in this mystery the Lord calls the early disciples to an awareness of the kingdom of God and through them, to use his own words to anyone 'with ears to hear'. In other words, we are all involved insofar as we choose to accept God's kingdom.

The Story Told

Most of Jesus' story-telling involved parables and most of his witness to the kingdom of God, is lived through miracles, healings, acts of kindness and forgiveness. In all he says and does, the Lord, draws us to the kingdom of God. It is not a geographical location but a state of mind, soul and heart that opens us to hear and respond to God's word.

The kingdom of God is like a man who finds a pearl in a field, goes sells everything he owns and buys the field, or a woman who lost a coin and spent the day searching for it and when she found it, invited people to celebrate. In another text, it is a shepherd leaving ninety-nine sheep to go in search of one that has strayed. Again, it is a celebration to which many have been invited but choose not to respond. It is like the wise and foolish ten waiting for their master's return – some with oil in their lamps and others with not enough. It is like a man coming to a neighbour in the night, looking for food because someone has called to him unexpectedly. It is a Good Samaritan who says yes, and a rich young man who wants to say yes but cannot bring himself. The kingdom of God is choice.

It is to be found in practically every word spoken by Jesus and is at the heart of his mission. He sought to draw people to a place of knowing and responding to God's love. Only when that truly happens, when the ends of the earth have been reached, when baptism has been celebrated, can the kingdom be fully alive and revealed. It is always a journey.

We are all asked to proclaim this kingdom in our life choices and through the encouragement of others. This mystery is included here to remind us that Jesus' primary role on earth was to invite people to God's kingdom, here on earth and hereafter. We recall the 'Good Thief' as he is called, who turned to Jesus on Calvary's hill and said: 'Jesus, remember me when you come into your kingdom', to which he received the reply: 'I promise you, this day you will be with me in paradise'.

The thief recognised the kingdom through Jesus – through his life and innocent death. It is only in Jesus and an acceptance of his message that we too can fully encounter that kingdom and, having done so, with Jesus we are asked to proclaim to all that the Kingdom of God is at hand and can only be reached through repentance and a resolve to turn away from all that is evil, destructive and not from God.

Thoughts for Prayer
Prayers for missionary men and women could well

accompany this mystery. Perhaps we know a missionary priest, sister or lay person so why not name them here and ask God's blessing on them as they seek to bring gospel values to other people. We might think of earthly kingdoms and states and pray for all in leadership, that they will recognise God's role in all our lives and speak less about separation of church and state, and more about gathering together all that is good and positive in both, so that people's lives might be enriched and society strengthened. We remember all who shaped us in our faith – once again we think of our own families, teachers, priests and religious in our parishes and schools and all who pointed us in the direction of Christ.

LUMINOUS MYSTERY 4
TRANSFIGURATION
(LK 9:28–36)

Who Is in the Story?
Peter, James and John are the key figures who often accompany Jesus at times when he wishes to share an insight and vision. We also encounter Moses and Elijah – a reminder that Jesus is the fulfilment of the promise made to them.

The Story Told
The climbing of a mountain is often linked with entering a space for prayer. The very imagery of climbing, perhaps,

represents our journey towards God and his willingness to come and meet us. Mountains feature a lot in Scripture and, in our own traditions, we know what it is to make pilgrimages to mountain tops. In the making of this prayer journey, Jesus brings with him Peter, James and John who seem to be favoured by him at moments like this. We recall his bringing the same three into the room of Jairus' daughter when he raised her from the dead and they were with him in the Garden of Gethsemane.

On the mountain top, Jesus is revealed to the three in a way they had never seen before. The description tell us that his clothes were dazzlingly white and his appearance brighter than any earthly bleacher could make it. Radiance shone from him and he stood in their midst in the company of Moses and Elijah. We recall that Elijah too, encountered God on the mountain top, as did Moses. Jesus speaks to these giants of the Old Testament, as if to friends, with Peter, James and John being awe-struck by the vision.

They, in their feeling that it is 'wonderful for us to be here', suggest building three tents to shelter Jesus and his companions who, at this stage, have vanished again. Jesus reminds the three that they cannot stay on the mountain but must live their lives on earth and make a difference there. Just as Moses came down from Sinai with the Ten Commandments, so must they return to their people and encourage them to live in accordance with God's will. He further reminds them that they are not to speak of this encounter, for it is intended for them to reassure them and open their eyes to his truth. He tells them they can speak of it after he is risen from the dead.

They keep this moment to themselves but wonder what he means in the reference to rising from the dead. Later, of course, they will understand the significance of that statement.

This is a powerful moment in Jesus' ministry, and we do well to reflect on it and let the story reach us again in reflecting on this mystery.

Thoughts for Prayer
We could reflect on pilgrimage here – remembering places like Lough Derg, Croagh Patrick, Lourdes, Fatima, Rome, Knock, the Holy Land. We could remember those making pilgrimage in the hope of a spiritual encounter. We remember people on the Camino, on the various caminos at home or on the well-known Camino de Santiago de Compostela. We might pray as well for the ability to see God as revealed to us in nature and life's moments. We could pray as well for a willingness to come down from the mountain and live out our faith on the everyday paths of our lives. There is a call to be grateful to God for sending his Son to be among us and lead us to a better place. Maybe there's place here too for a prayer for priests and religious, that they too might allow themselves be taken by the Lord to that place where he needs them to be so that his truth may be revealed.

LUMINOUS MYSTERY 5
THE INSTITUTION OF THE
EUCHARIST
(LK 22:14-20)

Who Is in the Story?
Jesus and the twelve apostles are the central characters. It is possible that others were there too, but dialogue recorded speaks to and around Jesus and the twelve.

The Story Told
It is the story that lies at the heart of our faith – Jesus offering himself to his apostles in the Eucharistic meal of 'The Last Supper'. Here, he takes the bread and wine, shares it at the table and declares it to be his body and blood. We are the gathered guests around that same table in the 'Upper Room' and we are found in every parish and every church where people gather to worship.

We find these words and actions repeated and relived in every celebration of the Mass and, in this, we 'proclaim his death and resurrection until he comes again'. We are the gathered guests around that same table in the 'Upper Room' as found in every parish and in every church where we gather to worship.

The word 'Eucharist' means thanksgiving and it is in that spirit of gratitude that we recall the institution of the Eucharist. We are reminded as well of the Lord's act of service when he washes the feet of his disciples and encourages them to do likewise for one another and for everyone. Eucharist is about receiving strength from the

Lord's own body and blood that we might be people of service – people of faith.

This mystery also reminds us of the uncertainty and reluctance that was found around that table. Peter did not want his feet washed and Judas left the table to betray the Lord. These actions serve to remind us that there will always be a struggle to grasp the full meaning of the Lord's role in our lives and that, for some, the journey is too much. We pray then for a deepening of our own awareness of Eucharist, its central place in our lives and hearts and of its power to give us the strength needed for the day to day living of our lives.

The Lord, throughout the Scriptures, sought to feed people. We are aware of his miracle of feeding the five thousand and know that one of the central ingredients in that miracle was bread. We recall that in the Old Testament story of Exodus, the fleeing Israelites were nourished each day by a bread-like substance (manna) that was provided by the Lord.

Finally, there is a call going out to us all through this mystery to be a Eucharistic people – a people rooted in thanksgiving for all the Lord has done for us and given to us.

Thoughts for Prayer

We might recall here our own First Holy Communion and the gratitude we felt on that day. We could remember other occasions when we felt nourished though Eucharist. There could be space here to pray for deepening of our reverence, a commitment to spend some time in

Eucharistic adoration and a prayer for priests that, in their celebrating Eucharist, they might always model their celebration on Jesus'. Pray too for people who have been confused in their faith or who have walked away from it, and for some who do not know how to return that they may come to know Jesus as 'the way, the truth and the life'.

CHAPTER 3
THE SORROWFUL MYSTERIES

Ordinarily these mysteries are prayed on Tuesday and Friday.

In the humanity of Jesus, all human emotion is experienced. Hence the sorrowful mysteries, for there is no denying that humanity experiences times of great sorrow, uncertainty and pain. These mysteries speak to these occasions and to an awareness that suffering is part of our journey.

The sorrowful mysteries are located in hours and days rather than months and years and take us from the moment Jesus left the Upper Room and Eucharistic Table, through the hours that passed from that moment and through Good Friday. Here we encounter the suffering Christ and, in our awareness of his suffering, we learn that perhaps he offers us most comfort when darkness descends on and around ourselves.

Here we will encounter friends who want to be supportive but can't fully find the words and who may even seem to sleep through our difficulties. We will find soldiers following orders and maybe losing some of their humanity and soul. Mockery too will make its appearance and remind us of the cruelty contained therein.

It must nonetheless be remembered that these mysteries come from the joyful and luminous moments of Jesus' life and, while they have their place and must be endured, they truly prepare the way for the glorious.

SORROWFUL MYSTERY 1
THE AGONY IN THE GARDEN
(LK 22:40–46)

Who Is in the Story?
Peter, James and John are chosen to accompany Jesus at this crucial moment. Judas makes an appearance at the end, accompanied by the soldiers and crowd.

The Story Told
Aware of all that was to unfold, Jesus chose to spend some time in prayer to prepare himself. As we will see in the Transfiguration, he asks Peter, James and John to accompany him and asks that they stay awake while he goes a little from them to pray. His prayer is one of petition. He asks God the Father, to spare him from this moment if possible but adds (echoing Mary's words in the Annunciation story) 'your will be done'. He describes his state as being 'sorrowful to the point of death' and clearly associates himself with all who have been in that dark place of doubt, anxiety and personal pain.

His prayer, though not answered in deliverance from the moment, is heard and strength is given. This same strength is not given to his companions who fall asleep while Jesus prays. He asks them why they slept and wonders why they could not watch with him. We are reminded here of people who watch with us in times of sorrow – maybe through the wake in our home or staff on night duty in a hospital. We know the value of companionship and the support offered through meaningful presence. This mystery is calling us to such awareness and a willingness to watch with him wherever and whenever someone is suffering and sorrowful.

This mystery speaks to the doubts we might well have about God's presence in our hour of need and why it is we cannot be delivered from difficult moments. The underlying message is that God is there, he will reassure and strengthen us for the rough road and will never abandon us. Gethsemane, with its agony, calls us to accept that God is there for us even when we find it difficult to believe and accept that reality.

Thoughts for Prayer
There may be room here to remember those who have been with us in difficult times and to offer a prayer of gratitude for support received. We might recall those who are facing into a difficult journey, possibly of medical treatments or surgical procedures. Maybe we locate ourselves in the garden, when we feel vulnerable and challenged, fearful and perplexed and ask God to send his angels to watch over us. We could pray in this mystery for acceptance of a difficult situation, in the knowledge that Jesus accompanies us in a very real way at this moment.

SORROWFUL MYSTERY 2
THE SCOURGING AT THE PILLAR
(JN 19:1)

Who Is in the Story?
Pilate, soldiers, Jesus and onlookers.

The Story Told
We know that Pilate had no desire to see Jesus crucified. Deep down, he knew there was nothing in Jesus' life that demanded his execution. Though he tried to release Jesus, he feared the crowd and ordered that Jesus be flogged. In many ways, it is at least possible, he felt this to be the better of two evils and hoped that it might be enough to satisfy his accusers and detractors. Maybe if they saw him suffer, that would be enough. The flogging was prolonged, painful and humiliating but sadly not enough.

In this mystery we see the flesh of Jesus torn asunder. This in sharp contrast to his own ministry where he smoothed leprous skin, straightened twisted hands, strengthened paralysed legs, opened blinded eyes, put sound in deafened ears – in short healed. This mystery reminds us of how easily we can slip into violence and especially when we are lost in a hostile group.

Here Jesus identifies and aligns himself to all who suffer torture and harassment. He calls out to those with whips and tools of torture in their hands and under their control to hear his screams, witness the brutality and to recoil from it.

This violence, rooted in man's inhumanity to man, is

not confined to a courtyard of two thousand years ago in Jerusalem, but is found all too frequently on our streets, in migrant ships, concentration camps and throughout society.

It was wrong then. It is wrong now. As Jesus said so many times; 'Listen, anyone who has ears to hear'.

Thoughts for Prayer
Some suffering is beyond our control – we think, for example, of sickness or bereavement. This mystery asks us to pray for those who suffer needlessly at the hands of others. We are called to pray for a deepening of our own social conscience and to let it be known we do not support or seek torture of any human being or animal. We pray for hearts that never become numb to the pain inflicted on others.

SORROWFUL MYSTERY 3
THE CROWNING WITH THORNS
(MK 15:17)

Who Is in the Story?
The suffering Christ.

The Story Told
Once again, decency is lost in the mob. Someone decided that it would be funny to mock Jesus and to pour doubt over his status as king. Though he claimed no geographical kingdom, as will be seen in the luminous mysteries, he

came to proclaim the kingdom. Pilate had questioned him about this and Jesus assured him that his kingdom was not of the type Pilate had in mind but, as 'king' he was 'born for this and came into the world for this' and, he added 'all who are on the side of truth, listen to my voice'. Pilate questioned him: 'What is truth?' (Jn 18:38) but Jesus made no answer. The answer to that question is personal and can only be arrived at through reflection.

The mob mentality allowed no room for reflection and the thorns, twisted into a crown were placed on the 'king's' head, pressed in so that their damage would be two-fold. Mark him as a fool and draw even more blood in the process.

Like the scourging, this mystery is rooted in violence done to the innocent. There is no justification for it and that really is the story told. Often there is no justification for the pressure we find ourselves burdened with. People do not deserve to suffer in the way that often befalls them and the crowd still has to come to self-awareness that it is not enough to stand idly by while people suffer.

There is possibly something being said here too about pressure of the mind. That crown of thorns is a feeling all too familiar to many and maybe Jesus is identifying here with those who suffer such pressure. He may well be calling out to us to untie twisted thorns, to share some of the pain but ultimately to restore people's peace of mind.

Thoughts for Prayer
A prayer for individual conviction that where we see wrong being done, we address it and distance ourselves

from it. We think again of victims of group violence and of people who have had property damaged when the mob rules the moment. There's room for prayer for those who feel the world tightening around their minds, darkness descending and hope vanishing. We might pray for those who might consider self-harm and pray for their deliverance.

SORROWFUL MYSTERY 4
THE CARRYING OF THE CROSS
(LK 22:40–46)

Who Is in the Story?
Jesus, soldiers, on-lookers, disciples, women of Jerusalem, Mary, Simon (and from Stations of the Cross, Veronica)

The Story Told
It is a story of the final climb to Calvary. The 'cross', a symbol of suffering is placed on Jesus' shoulders and the journey begins. Along the way he is given the forced help of Simon of Cyrene who is dragged from the crowd.

Jesus' falls along the way speak to us of frailty and human weakness and of being able to endure only so much. Three falls are alluded to – the first unwelcome and unexpected and the other two more painful because they happened before. The falls of Jesus, in a strange way it seems, are an encouragement to people to keep getting up and to focus on the desire to get up rather than dwell on the falls. 'How many times must I forgive?' 'Not seven, but seventy times seven …' (Mt 18:22).

The 'cross' itself speaks of burdens carried and quite often undeserved and certainly un-invited. Jesus transforms the cross into a bridge between earth and heaven, death and life, despair and hope, failure and triumph, loss and gain. We are reminded that the cross was left behind and that, even at its most cruel moment, it became a source of salvation for a repentant thief and of conversion for a soldier.

We are asked not to be burdened by the cross but to be liberated through it. Leonard Cohen, in a wonderful song called 'Come healing', speaks of the cross in these words: 'The splinters that we carry, the cross we left behind, come healing of the body, come healing of the mind'. The carrying of the cross is a call to a deeper faith in the power of healing.

Thoughts for Prayer

There may be room here to remember those who have been with us in difficult times and to offer a prayer of gratitude for support received. We might recall those who are facing into a difficult journey, possibly of medical treatments or surgical procedures. Maybe we locate ourselves in the garden, when we feel vulnerable and challenged, fearful and perplexed and ask God to send his Angels to watch over us. We could pray in this mystery for acceptance of a difficult situation, in the knowledge that Jesus accompanies us in a very real way at this moment.

SORROWFUL MYSTERY 5
THE CRUCIFIXION
(MT 27:32–56)

Who Is in the Story?
Jesus, two thieves, soldiers, Mary, John, the disciples, jeering crowd and, quite likely, silent and sad well-wishers.

The Story Told
There is a lot of detail given around the crucifixion of Jesus and, though the soldiers thought it was the end of the journey, it showed itself to be the beginning.

It was a slow and painful process where dignity was stripped away. On Calvary's hill, Jesus hung on the cross for three hours and, during that time was mocked by many. People, yet again caught up in the mob mentality, screamed at him for a display of power – 'If you are the Christ … ', 'He saved others, let him save himself', 'Hail, King of the Jews' and so it went.

There were moments when Jesus reached into the crowd and spoke to those who had 'ears to hear' – most notably his mother and the beloved disciple, John. To John he entrusted the care of Our Lady and to her, the care of the beloved disciple. From that moment a place was made for her in John's home. He spoke also with one of those crucified with him – a man who rose above the jeers, including those of the third man being executed. This man had called on Jesus to save them all from the cross – from death – if he was who he claimed to be. The other man realised that there was more at stake than being saved from death. He saw, in Jesus, the way to salvation and prayed 'Jesus, remember me when you come into your kingdom'. The response was swift and sincere, 'This day, you will be with me in paradise' (Lk 23:43).

As in Gethsemane, Jesus calls again to his father and does so from a place where he feels abandoned – 'My God, my God, why have you forsaken me?' (Mt 27:46). This prayer serves as a reminder that even though he felt forsaken, he did not lose faith and still called to God. There is something being said about justifiable anger and about being tested to the limit but all the while, retaining belief in God's presence with us, even on the darkest day.

Among the words spoken by Jesus are two that cry out to us from the depths of his heart: 'I thirst!' The soldiers mockingly satisfied his thirst with a soaked sponge of vinegar but that is not the thirst he is calling us to recognise. He wants us to know he thirsts for us and, one soldier without sponge or vinegar was among the first to satisfy that thirst for, having seen how Jesus died, he declared: 'In truth, this man was a son of God' (Mt 27:54).

At the moment of Jesus' death, we are told the veil of the temple was torn in two from top to bottom and this speaks of the veil that divided the everyday man and woman in the temple from those considered holy and honoured. The veil hung before the sanctuary and only the elect could go beyond it. Others could not see what lay beyond it. Now there are no barriers. Jesus' crucifixion and death on the cross open for one and all the way to come into God's presence.

We look for moments of kindness too, in this mystery

and remember Joseph of Arimathea who offered to have the body of Jesus buried in a tomb he had marked out for himself. The women who took notice of where he was buried and later would return to anoint his body. Even Pilate who had the sign erected over the Cross of Jesus 'The King of The Jews' sought to make a public statement that he knew who it was that had stood, falsely accused, before him. When asked to amend this sign, Pilate refused, saying: 'What I have written, I have written' (Jn 19:22).

The shadow of Calvary gave way to the glory of God and we must cling to the hope, even at our darkest hour, that 'this too will pass'.

Thoughts for Prayer
A prayer for the dying could well accompany this decade. We could remember too the call to repentance, even at the twelfth hour. We might give thanks for those who come to welcome Jesus into their lives when all hope seems to have gone. We remember all who grieve the loss of a loved one and give thanks for people's kindness and support as we think of Joseph of Arimathea and others who saw what others could not see.

CHAPTER FOUR
THE GLORIOUS MYSTERIES

*These mysteries are ordinarily prayed
on Sunday and Wednesday.*

The glorious mysteries take us through the key moments following the discovery of the empty tomb on Easter Sunday morning. They remind us of Jesus' promise to his disciples that he would be with them (with us) always, 'yes, to the end of time' and of the promised sending of the Holy Spirit.

The final two mysteries speak of Our Lady being drawn up to heaven where she is declared its queen as well as queen of the earth.

These mysteries are the launching pad for the Church as a people of faith, who unlike Thomas believe without seeing and rely on the writings of Scripture and the nourishment of the sacraments for their guiding principles.

The glorious mysteries are a foretaste of all that awaits the believing man and woman and are intended to be our guide and encouragement in our day to day life.

GLORIOUS MYSTERY 1
THE RESURRECTION
(LK 24)

Who Is in the Story?

Angels, Mary Magdalene, Mary the mother of James, Joanna, Peter, John, the disciples on the road to Emmaus and Jesus.

The Story Told

There was unfinished business from Good Friday evening and the women, who had carefully taken note of where and how Jesus was buried, returned to the tomb to do for him what haste would not allow for on Friday evening. Namely, to anoint his body in accordance with tradition. It was an honourable course of action and one well and rightly recorded in the gospel passage(s).

They arrived to find the stone – the same stone they had talked about on their way to the tomb, rolled away. At first panic sets in, and as they go to the tomb they discover it to be empty. Horror strikes them as they think the body of Jesus has been stolen but then they receive a vision of angels who assure them this is not the case and who question why they look among the dead for one who is alive. 'He is not here. He is risen'. In a state of alarm they rush to tell the apostles and Peter and John run to the tomb. They too are shocked and at a loss, but gradually his words come back to them – that he 'must rise from the dead.'

There are a few accounts of what happened around this

event and one sees Mary encounter a man she supposes to be a gardener and when he asks what is wrong she tells him she thinks the body of Jesus has been stolen. She asks the man, if he knows where it is so that she might go and carry it back to the tomb. The next word is wonderful: 'Mary' – and, in the tone of voice she recognises him for who he is, the Risen Saviour.

Later in the day Jesus encounters two of the disciples on a seven mile walk away from Jerusalem. 'What matters are you discussing as you walk along?' he asks, and we know that he enters a conversation with them that leads them to a shared table, broken bread and moment of recognition in the village of Emmaus.

What is being said to us, in this mystery, is that the acceptance of Jesus' resurrection from the dead is key but that it is a gradual journey, involving conversation with Christ that he may speak to the depths of our hearts and, awaken there, love of him and an acceptance of his message.

Thoughts for Prayer

We could pray around a deepening of our own faith in the resurrection. We allow ourselves be caught up in conversation, like Mary and the disciples on the Emmaus road, with Jesus so that he might speak to us too and bring us that place where we recognise 'our hearts burning within us as he talks to us on the road and explains the scriptures to us'.

GLORIOUS MYSTERY 2
THE ASCENSION
(LK 24:31 AND ACTS 1:1–11)

Who Is in the Story?
Jesus, Mary and the apostles.

The Story Told
On the outskirts of Jerusalem Jesus gathers with the apostles. The hill of Calvary seemed to take Jesus from them and now, another hill (the Mount of Olives, close to where he experienced the uncertainty of the Garden of Gethsemane) sees him taken from them again but in a different way. Here, he is in control of the moment whereas Calvary was in the control of people with evil intent. There is however, sorrow and uncertainty for the apostles on both hills.

Jesus reassures the apostles that this moment has to come and unless he goes from them, in this way, the Holy Spirit cannot enter their lives to that depth where it needs to reside, transform and empower them.

As he is taken from them, they look to the skies and wonder. The angels respond to this wonder as on Easter Sunday, and bring them to a clearer understanding that this moment must happen. They are told, and through them, we are told that Christ will return as we have seen him go.

The apostles are commissioned to go to the ends of the earth, proclaiming the kingdom and sharing baptism with those encountered.

A prayer here for missionary men and women who have taken to heart the Lord's final instruction. We pray too that we may have the courage and conviction to proclaim our faith in the day to day living of our lives. We might remember as well those who have had to let go of someone they love, possibly through separation or loss of a friendship and pray that they may encounter healing, peace of mind and that, where possible, reconciliation might take place.

GLORIOUS MYSTERY 3
THE DESCENT OF THE HOLY SPIRIT
(ACTS 2:1-11)

Who Is in the Story?
The apostles, and those in the upper room, including of course, Mary, the mother of Jesus; visitors to Jerusalem and The Holy Spirit.

The Story Told
A locked room is the location for this mystery. Here, the apostles and disciples gathered and were joined in continuous prayer by Mary the mother of Jesus. Their prayer was for strength and guidance and for an acceptance of where Jesus wanted them to go – to the ends of the earth, but they could not bring themselves to leave a locked room. The end of the earth was a long

way off for them. Their prayer was to be answered in an incredible way.

The Holy Spirit entered that locked room. More than that, the Holy Spirit entered their hearts and souls and unlocked, not just the door, but the wonder of their ministry.

They left behind the locked room, headed for the street and there encountered a people searching for answers and seeking a way. They spoke to these people, addressing them in their own language so that the word of Christ could be understood by all. The people from many places represent the peoples of the world and the speaking of many languages reminds us that the Gospel too must be proclaimed in language accessible to all.

This mystery celebrates the birth of the Church and the wonder of this day is recalled in the Sacrament of Confirmation when the words spoken are simple but powerful: 'Be sealed with the gifts of the Holy Spirit' and 'Peace be with you'.

It is a story of beginning.

Thoughts for Prayer

An openness to the promptings of the Holy Spirit could well be our prayer in this mystery. Here, we might look for what are sometimes called 'the signs of the times' to see what the 'Spirit may be saying to the Church' – saying to you and me. We might reflect on the gifts and fruits of the Holy Spirit as encountered and gifted to us on our Confirmation day, give thanks and seek ways to best utilise these. Maybe a prayer to find the strength and faith to unlock those doors that, all too often, hold us back from reaching our full potential.

The final two glorious mysteries are not so much referred to directly in Scripture as alluded to in some of the biblical passages. They are teachings of our faith and accepted as such through faith. They remind us that Our Lady's first 'yes', encountered in the first joyful mystery, found many echoes throughout her life and that it was singularly rewarded in her being drawn into Heaven to be in the company of the saints and in the presence of the Trinity. From here, she continues to echo and encourage that 'yes' in all of us.

GLORIOUS MYSTERY 4
THE ASSUMPTION

Who Is in the Story?
Our Lady.

The Story Told
In what is seen as the ending and reward for a life truly given to God, Mary is assumed into Heaven, body and soul. At her conception, she was free of the legacy of sin passed on to us all, and now the body which gave birth to her son is brought into heaven.

In her assumption, Mary brings with her the needs of the world and continues to intercede for people, witnessing to their needs and responding.

Mary's witness, as recorded in the Knock Apparition

of 1879, speaks well to the truth of her nature. Standing silently, in the company of Joseph and the beloved disciple John, to whose care she was committed on Calvary, she points toward the altar and there, the Lamb of God. She continues to see herself in the role of 'The handmaid of the Lord' and encourages us to always acknowledge God, turn towards him in prayer and to give thanks.

The Assumption then is not a farewell or a removal from our midst but a continuation of a relationship that sees Mary noticing people's needs, responding to them and seeking always to do God's will.

Thoughts for Prayer
A prayer around gratitude for Mary's 'yes' that paved the way for the coming of Christ. We might remember our own mothers too; and give thanks for their many acts of selflessness. We could pray for a blessing of family life and for healing where there is division or unhappiness.

GLORIOUS MYSTERY 5
THE CORONATION OF OUR LADY

Who Is in the Story
Everybody!

The Story Told
The final glorious mystery is a call to us to recognise the role played by Mary in our salvation. She has been aligned with Jesus from that moment Gabriel brought to her the

news of her being chosen. Not for a single second did she allow herself to be distracted from the mission assigned to her and, though aware it would cause her pain, she never turns her back on what God asked of her.

On a personal note, I like to think more of Mary as mother than queen. Like most people, I would not feel particularly comfortable in the presence of a queen and would find myself very self-conscious. On the other hand, I had no such feelings in the company of my own mother – I knew where I stood with her and I knew for certain, the love she had for me. I believe Our Lady knew the hard life too and that she walked many of the paths we travel and endured her own moments of uncertainty, pain and disappointment. This, to me, makes her very real and very accessible.

Yes, in this mystery we honour and acclaim her as 'Queen of Heaven and Earth' but we don't lose sight of the woman in the home, the woman on the street, the woman at the wedding reception or the woman at the foot of the cross. Neither do we forget the one joined with the apostles in continuous prayer and, from all this awareness of Mary as constant companion, we can too accept her as queen – one deserving respect and one who has the interests of her people, of all people, firmly lodged in her loving heart and gentle ways.

Thoughts for Prayer
That we might become more aware of our connectedness with heaven. We might pray for a deepened awareness of Mary as 'advocate' and mother, knowing that she cares

deeply for our needs. We might find time to thank Mary for noticing the many times we were without 'wine' and for her ability to remind Jesus of our needs.

CONCLUSION

Going back to Dick Farrelly's Isle of Inisfree and memories of his family at prayer, we might do our best to create memories for future generations. Truly the family and the home at prayer are both a gift and a joy to behold.

In 'telling' the Rosary, we are mindful of the days aligned with different mysteries but there may well be a place and space for taking mysteries 'out of sync' and allowing them speak to our heart on a given day or in a particular situation. Sometimes too, it can be good to take a decade or two from different sets of mysteries if and when they allow us to connect with something within that needs special attention.

At days' end, the telling of the Rosary is the telling of Christ's story and Mary's place in that is to be the story-teller and the one who points us, as at Knock, towards the Lamb of God.

I remember when growing up, a priest in my home parish used to speak a lot about Our Lady and he had a prayer that he learned from someone else – a simple prayer of intercession through Mary. I liked it:

> *You can't say you can't*
> *and you won't say you won't*
> *so you will, won't you?*
> *Amen.*

SO IT'S TOLD

The announcement brought yes
visitation, a chance to bless;
the birth brought news of greatest joy
presentation recognised the God sent boy
the Temple finding after loss,
foretaste of Calvary's wooden cross.

Jordan's water had to pour
Cana's water to wine brought more,
Kingdom come and will be done
on mountain top revealed as Son;
take and drink, take and eat
in my memory to all you meet.

Tears shed with heavy heart
at pillar flesh was torn apart;
crown of thorns bring blood to face
a cross un-deserved is put in place;
one thought forsaken wonders why
on darkened hill he has to die.

Stone rolled back and empty tomb
risen to enter the Heavenly room;
Spirit sent to nourish all,
Reward for Mary's 'yes' to call;
Queen of Heaven, Queen of Earth,
the mother who shared the Saviour's birth.

(Vincent Sherlock, July 2019)